TREE
of
WONDER

The Many Marvelous Lives of a Rainforest Tree

by KATE MESSNER

illustrated by SIMONA MULAZZANI

chronicle books · san francisco

1

Deep in the forest, in the warm-wet green, ONE ALMENDRO TREE grows, stretching its branches toward sun.

Among these gnarled roots and rutted bark, crisscrossed limbs and rain-drenched leaves, a whole hidden world bustles and thrives.

*A single **ALMENDRO TREE** can produce more than a million flowers when it blooms. Later, animals will come from all over the forest to eat the fruit that it bears. Many others are already here, hidden in the shadows and leaves, and depend on the tree not just for food but for a home. In all, more than a thousand different living things depend on this tree.*

Look up—way up! GREAT GREEN MACAWS
nest in the hollow left by a fallen branch.
Soon, there will be more!

2

Flocks of **GREAT GREEN MACAWS** will come to feast on the almendro's ripe fruit, but it's likely that just one couple will make its home in the tree. Great Green Macaws, or lapas verdes *as they are known in Latin America, mate for life and return to the same nest hole each year. They lay eggs and raise chicks in the almendro tree, drink water that collects in the tree's cavities, and feast on fruit as it ripens.*

5

Who's hungry? KEEL-BILLED TOUCANS
bawk and squawk and squabble over breakfast.

4

KEEL-BILLED TOUCANS *often travel in flocks of four to twelve birds. They're easy to recognize by the colorful bills they use to pick fruit. Toucans sometimes use their bills to toss fruit to one another, as if they're playing a game.*

What's that growly, roaring sound?
HOWLER MONKEYS swing
and balance, chasing each other
from branch to branch. *"Tag, you're
it!" "That fruit is MINE!"*

HOWLER MONKEYS *usually live in troops, groups that range from just a few to nearly twenty. They are the largest—and loudest—monkeys in Latin America. Male howler monkeys have extra-large throats and vocal chambers so powerful their call can be heard 3 miles (5 kilometres) away. They're telling other monkeys, "This territory is taken by our troop, so keep moving!" When howler monkeys take fruit from the almendro tree, they sometimes carry it away and drop their leftovers on the ground, spreading seeds. In this way, the almendro tree feeds the monkeys and the forest, all at once.*

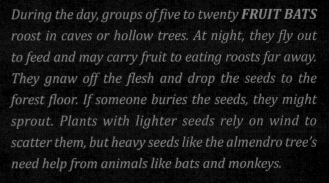

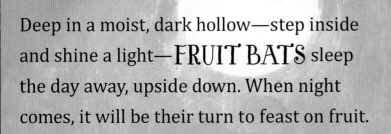

Deep in a moist, dark hollow—step inside and shine a light—FRUIT BATS sleep the day away, upside down. When night comes, it will be their turn to feast on fruit.

*During the day, groups of five to twenty **FRUIT BATS** roost in caves or hollow trees. At night, they fly out to feed and may carry fruit to eating roosts far away. They gnaw off the flesh and drop the seeds to the forest floor. If someone buries the seeds, they might sprout. Plants with lighter seeds rely on wind to scatter them, but heavy seeds like the almendro tree's need help from animals like bats and monkeys.*

Watch where you fly, fruit bats. . . .
FER-DE-LANCE vipers—
a mother and her newborn
babies—lurk, curled and coiled,
waiting for prey.

32

🐍 🐍 🐍 🐍 🐍
🐍 🐍 🐍 🐍 🐍
🐍 🐍 🐍 🐍 🐍
🐍 🐍 🐍 🐍 🐍
🐍 🐍 🐍 🐍 🐍
🐍 🐍 🐍 🐍 🐍
🐍 🐍

*A female **FER-DE-LANCE** may give birth to more than fifty live young snakes at a time, each one about 1 foot (30 centimetres) long. The fer-de-lance loves fallen branches and rotten logs on the forest floor. Females are larger than males and can grow to be 8 feet (2.4 metres) long. Even the babies can give a painful and dangerous bite. Toxic venom and an aggressive attitude make the fer-de-lance the deadliest snake in Costa Rica.*

13

Someone else is searching
for food. . . . AGOUTIS sniff
and snuffle the forest floor.
They gorge on fallen fruit.
Then gather! Dig! Gather more!
Agoutis stockpile food, hiding
it away for later.

64

AGOUTIS usually live in small family groups but may gather in groups of up to a hundred to feed. These animals help the almendro tree by collecting its seeds and burying them in secret stashes all over the forest, the same way squirrels might bury acorns in your lawn. Scientists say these animals are "scatter hoarding," hiding food in many places so that if another animal discovers one hiding spot, there will still be plenty of food left. Agoutis bury so much food they can't keep track of it all, and some of those forgotten seeds grow into new almendro trees.

Someone's playing hide-and-seek. . . .

BLUE MORPHO BUTTERFLIES

flutter through leaves on electric blue
wings and then land—brown-bark
invisible—on the trunk.

A single almendro tree can easily supply food for more than a hundred **BLUE MORPHO BUTTERFLIES**. Blue Morphos sip the juice from the fruit of the almendro tree after it falls and begins to rot. Scientists believe these butterflies may deter predators by roosting in groups, flashing their bright blue wings to surprise them, and by folding up their wings so the brown side blends in with tree bark and leaf litter. The wings even have eye markings to make the butterfly resemble the face of an owl or a hawk.

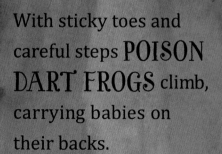

With sticky toes and careful steps POISON DART FROGS climb, carrying babies on their backs.

256

Male **POISON DART FROGS** gather in large groups before mating. Then, each female lays up to five or six eggs on the forest floor. Once the tadpoles hatch, their parents give them a piggyback ride, one or two at a time, up into a tree. Almendro trees are home to many air plants, or bromeliads, which catch and hold pools of water in the rainforest downpours. Here, the tadpoles are safer from predators than they would be on the ground.

512

✶✶✶✶✶✶✶✶✶✶✶✶✶✶✶✶✶✶✶✶✶✶✶✶✶✶✶✶✶✶✶✶
✶✶✶✶✶✶✶✶✶✶✶✶✶✶✶✶✶✶✶✶✶✶✶✶✶✶✶✶✶✶✶✶
✶✶✶✶✶✶✶✶✶✶✶✶✶✶✶✶✶✶✶✶✶✶✶✶✶✶✶✶✶✶✶✶
✶✶✶✶✶✶✶✶✶✶✶✶✶✶✶✶✶✶✶✶✶✶✶✶✶✶✶✶✶✶✶✶
✶✶✶✶✶✶✶✶✶✶✶✶✶✶✶✶✶✶✶✶✶✶✶✶✶✶✶✶✶✶✶✶
✶✶✶✶✶✶✶✶✶✶✶✶✶✶✶✶✶✶✶✶✶✶✶✶✶✶✶✶✶✶✶✶
✶✶✶✶✶✶✶✶✶✶✶✶✶✶✶✶✶✶✶✶✶✶✶✶✶✶✶✶✶✶✶✶
✶✶✶✶✶✶✶✶✶✶✶✶✶✶✶✶✶✶✶✶✶✶✶✶✶✶✶✶✶✶✶✶
✶✶✶✶✶✶✶✶✶✶✶✶✶✶✶✶✶✶✶✶✶✶✶✶✶✶✶✶✶✶✶✶
✶✶✶✶✶✶✶✶✶✶✶✶✶✶✶✶✶✶✶✶✶✶✶✶✶✶✶✶✶✶✶✶
✶✶✶✶✶✶✶✶✶✶✶✶✶✶✶✶✶✶✶✶✶✶✶✶✶✶✶✶✶✶✶✶
✶✶✶✶✶✶✶✶✶✶✶✶✶✶✶✶✶✶✶✶✶✶✶✶✶✶✶✶✶✶✶✶
✶✶✶✶✶✶✶✶✶✶✶✶✶✶✶✶✶✶✶✶✶✶✶✶✶✶✶✶✶✶✶✶
✶✶✶✶✶✶✶✶✶✶✶✶✶✶✶✶✶✶✶✶✶✶✶✶✶✶✶✶✶✶✶✶
✶✶✶✶✶✶✶✶✶✶✶✶✶✶✶✶✶✶✶✶✶✶✶✶✶✶✶✶✶✶✶✶
✶✶✶✶✶✶✶✶✶✶✶✶✶✶✶✶✶✶✶✶✶✶✶✶

But not every crevice is safe.
RUSTY WANDERING SPIDERS
venture out from their mother's care.
They'll build lairs of their own. . . .
and wait for dinner.

*After mating, a female **RUSTY WANDERING SPIDER** can lay hundreds of eggs in a sac that she'll carry until it's time for her babies to hatch. Not all of those eggs will develop into spiders, but those that do will likely attach a dragline to the plant and drop down to find a lower leaf for its lair.*

Rusty wandering spiders find many places to hide on an almendro tree, tucked inside leaves where insects come for shelter. Some large wandering spiders even hunt frogs by sensing the vibrations produced when frogs make courtship calls.

Beneath on the forest floor,
LEAFCUTTER ANTS
hurry-scurry over twisted roots,
hauling cargo over their backs.

1,024

✳✳
✳✳
✳✳
✳✳
✳✳
✳✳
✳✳
✳✳
✳✳
✳✳
✳✳
✳✳
✳✳
✳✳
✳✳
✳✳
✳✳
✳✳
✳✳
✳✳
✳✳
✳✳
✳✳

LEAFCUTTER ANTS *live in underground colonies that range from several dozen to more than three or four million. These ants don't eat the leaves they collect. Instead, the ants take them to their nests, chew them up, and use them to feed the fungus they grow for their own meals. A single ant colony can strip a tree of its leaves in one day. But the ants rotate the plants they visit, so they rarely kill a whole tree. These ants take from the almendro tree, but they also give something back. When the ants cut holes in the canopies of other trees, light shines through the forest so new almendro trees can grow.*

Life multiplies again and again . . .
in this ONE ALMENDRO TREE.

The Almendro Tree

In Latin America, the almendro tree is known as the "tree of life," and for good reason. A single almendro tree can be home to more than a thousand different kinds of organisms. But this tree's strength has also been its downfall. Because the almendro tree has very hard, termite-resistant wood, many trees have been cut for lumber. Others are felled to make room for plantations.

If you'd like to help protect macaws and other animals that rely on Latin America's rainforest trees, including the almendro, you might consider working with your class or a community group to raise money for an environmental organization working toward this goal.

The **Rainforest Biodiversity Group** is an organization based out of Wisconsin that works to protect biodiversity in the areas where Great Green Macaws nest. RBG volunteers work with landowners in Costa Rica to plant trees, monitor wildlife populations, create preserves, and provide education about the importance of biodiversity.

www.rainforestbiodiversity.org

The **World Parrot Trust**, an organization dedicated to protecting wild parrots all over the world, has set up a special fund to help the endangered Great Green Macaw. The money is being used for field work, habitat protection, and local education efforts.

www.parrots.org/index.php/ourwork/greatgreenmacaw/

Osa Conservation is a nonprofit organization dedicated to protecting the globally significant biodiversity of the Osa Peninsula, Costa Rica. The Osa is home to one of the healthiest populations of Scarlet Macaws in Central America as well as the largest remaining lowland Pacific rainforest between California and Colombia. NRDC has partnered with Osa Conservation to revive a rainforest and help keep Costa Rica's Osa Peninsula wild for Scarlet Macaws, howler monkeys, and other wildlife.

www.osaconservation.org

Rainforest Math

Did you notice that the numbers in this book double each time you turn a page? Rainforest animals multiply quickly! Here are some more rainforest math problems for you to try. The more howler monkeys you see next to a word problem, the more challenging it will be!

Difficulty:

1. There are four Great Green Macaws shown in the illustration on pages 4–5. When the eggs hatch, how many birds will there be all together?

2. There are four toucans in the illustration on pages 6–7. If each toucan eats 2 pieces of fruit, how many pieces of fruit will they eat all together?

Difficulty:

3. The howler monkeys in this book are traveling in a troop of 8. If this group meets 3 other groups the same size, things will get awfully loud! How many howler monkeys will there be then?

4. Fruit bats from 4 different caves fly to the almendro tree one night to feed. If 1 cave has 12 fruit bats, 2 caves have 15 bats each, and 1 cave has 19 bats, how many bats will there be when they all come together?

Difficulty:

5. Imagine that each of the 64 agoutis in this book buries 10 almendro seeds one morning. If the agoutis find half of those seeds later and eat them, how many seeds will be left in the ground and might sprout?

6. If each of the 256 poison dart frogs in this book have 5 tadpoles, how many tadpoles will there be? Rusty wandering spiders and other predators will eat some of them! If only half survive, how many will be left to grow into frogs?

7. Leafcutter ants in a colony have different jobs. Some are in charge of collecting leaves. Some guard the collectors. Some chew the leaves back at the nest, and some tend the growing fungus. If half of the 1,024 ants in the sidebar on page 23 are collectors, one fourth are guards, one eighth are leaf chewers, and one eighth are fungus farmers, how many ants are in each job group?

8. The mother fer-de-lance on page 12 has 31 babies. If those baby snakes are all female and each one grows up to have 48 babies of her own, how many snakes will there be all together? (Don't forget to include the original mother snake and her babies!)

9. Go back through the book and add up the animals in the sidebars, starting with 2 Great Green Macaws and ending with 1,024 leafcutter ants. How many animals are living on and around the tree in this book? If all almendro trees had the same number of animals, how many would you find on 2 trees? How about 10? How many animals would live on 100 almendro trees?

---

1. 6 macaws once the eggs hatch

2. 8 pieces of fruit

3. 32 howler monkeys

4. 61 fruit bats

5. 320 seeds

6. 1,280 tadpoles, 640 grow into frogs

7. 512 collectors, 256 guards, 128 leaf chewers, and 128 fungus farmers

8. 1,520 fer-de-lance snakes

9. 2,046 animals living on and around 1 tree, 4,092 animals on 2 trees, 20,460 animals on 10 trees, 204,600 animals on 100 trees

If you'd like to learn more about rainforests, the almendro tree, and the animals that call it home, check out these resources.

Read

A is for Anaconda: A Rainforest Alphabet by Anthony D. Fredericks, illustrated by Laura Regan. Sleeping Bear Press, 2009.

Over in the Jungle: A Rainforest Rhyme by Marianne Berkes, illustrated by Jeanette Canyon. Dawn Publications, 2007.

Rain Forest (DK Eye Wonder) by Elinor Greenwood. DK Publishing, 2001.

Tropical Rainforests by Seymour Simon. Harper-Collins, 2010.

Watch

Almendro: Tree of Life, a documentary written by Barbara Puskas and Ina Knobloch. Universum, 2003.

For Maddie, Alex, and Kaitlynn with love —*K. M.*
A Margherita—*S. M.*

Text copyright © 2015 by Kate Messner.
Illustrations copyright © 2015 by Simona Mulazzani.

NRDC

A portion of the proceeds from the sale of this book goes to support
the work of the Natural Resources Defense Council (NRDC).

Library of Congress Cataloging-in-Publication Data:
Messner, Kate.
 Tree of wonder / by Kate Messner ; illustrated by Simona Mulazzani.
   pages cm
 Other title: NRDC : tree of wonder
 Audience: 5-8.
 Audience: K to grade 3
 ISBN 978-1-4521-1248-0 (alk. paper)
 1. Rain forest ecology—Juvenile literature. 2. Habitat (Ecology)—
Juvenile literature. 3. Dipteryx oleifera—Juvenile literature. I. Mulazzani,
Simona, illustrator. II. Title. III. Title: NRDC : tree of wonder.
 QH541.5.R27M47 2015
 577.34—dc23

                    2013032910

Manufactured in China.

Design by Jennifer Tolo Pierce.
Typeset in Cambria and Garden.
The illustrations in this book were rendered in
acrylic and pencil on paper.

10 9 8 7 6 5 4 3 2 1

Chronicle Books LLC
680 Second Street
San Francisco, California 94107

Chronicle Books—we see things differently. Become part
of our community at www.chroniclekids.com.